SUNBEAMS AND DAYDREAMS

Edited by

Becki Mee

First published in Great Britain in 1999 by
POETRY NOW
Remus House,
Coltsfoot Drive,
Woodston,
Peterborough, PE2 9JX
Telephone (01733) 898101
Fax (01733) 313524

All Rights Reserved

Copyright Contributors 1999

HB ISBN 0 75430 723 9
SB ISBN 0 75430 724 7

FOREWORD

Although we are a nation of poets we are accused of not reading poetry, or buying poetry books. After many years of listening to the incessant gripes of poetry publishers, I can only assume that the books they publish, in general, are books that most people do not want to read.

Poetry should not be obscure, introverted, and as cryptic as a crossword puzzle: it is the poet's duty to reach out and embrace the world.

The world owes the poet nothing and we should not be expected to dig and delve into a rambling discourse searching for some inner meaning.

The reason we write poetry (and almost all of us do) is because we want to communicate: an ideal; an idea; or a specific feeling. Poetry is as essential in communication, as a letter; a radio; a telephone, and the main criteria for selecting the poems in this anthology is very simple: they communicate.

CONTENTS

Little Ragged Robin	Joan Patrickson	1
Wagtail	Evelyn Balmain	2
Wake, Beautiful Rose (A Villanelle)	David Barrow	3
A Garden In Spring	Adrianne Jones	4
Capricious Spring	Barbara Fosh	5
The Longing	D M Anderson	6
Beautiful Spring	Joan Taylor	7
Happy Rest Amid Glorous View	Marjorie Cowan	8
Fresh Vibes For All	Julie Powell	9
Kaleidoscope	Susan Goldsmith	10
Spring 1986	Carolyn Smith	11
Earth's Resurrection	Linda M Crook	12
Splash Of Spring Colour	Hilary Jill Robson	13
Can Spring Be Far Behind?	E M Spencer	14
Stirring Of Hope	Joan R Gilmour	15
Spring	Geoffrey Ackroyd	16
A Dream Of Spring	T Harris	17
Seasons Change	Joan M Emmens	18
Springtime	Eileen Burton	19
New Beginnings	Shirley Ann Lewis	20
Spring	Becky Robinson	21
Looking Forward	Joan Hands	22
What Spring Inspires	Karen Bailey	23
Springtime	Helga I Dharmpaul	24
Sunny Days	Anna King	25
Preceding Spring	Joan Page	26
Blossom Tree	Jane Smith	27
Spring Song	Rosetta Stone	28
Springtime	May Kay	29
Heaven's Country	David Bridgewater	30
Recollection	Pat Jones	31
Conscious Threshold	Gemma Parkes	32
Spring Has Sprung	Derrick Evers	33

Title	Author	Page
A Meal-Shared	Pat Heppel	34
Portraits In Lace	Emma Louise Taylor	35
The Five Senses Of Spring	Susan Skye	36
Wonderful Spring!	Janet Hewitt	37
Fresh Sap Surging	M Scroggs	38
Smells Like Spring	Louise C Fletcher	39
The Gift Of Easter	Joy M Jordan	40
February 14th	Daphne Rance	41
Seem Smell And Listen To Spring	Elizabeth (Burke) Mayes	42
Almond Blossom	R D Hiscoke	43
Beautiful Spring	Alma Montgomery Frank	44
Beautiful Spring!	Jane Rennie	45
SAD	Dennis Walker	46
Joy	Gez Larkin	47
Spring	Ida Dunwoodie	48
Spring, March 1999	U Johnson	49
Noticing Spring	Edmund Humphreys	50
'Passion'-Ate?	Dulcie Levene	51
Bearer Of The Sperm	Shirley Sammout	52
The Celandine	Paddy Jupp	53
Spring	Barbara Ann Barker	54
Yesterday's Pizza	Tom Ritchie	55
SOS On Earth	R Glendenning	56
Outside In Spring	Naomi Elisa Price	58
The Cat And Toad Welcoming Party	Gillian Fisher	59
Springtime	Margaret Poole	60
A Dream Of Spring!	Rebecca Henley	61
Stirling Harbour By Night	Martin Boddie	62
Something New!	Geoff O'Neil	63
Spirit Of The May	Catherine Reay	64
Dark To Light	Joanne Clarke	65
Untitled	Kathleen Reid	66
Promise Of Spring	Nan Ogg	67
Petals	Margaret Leigh	68
Spring Days	Rowland Ablett	69
Polaroid	Chris Blackmore	70

Springtime Melody	Rosemary Remy	71
Onward!	Seán Rooney	72
To Peg, Who Died on 20th June 1996	A F L Adams	73
Blossoms Of The Spring	A R Williams	74
I Dream Of Spring	Antonio Martorelli	75
A Dream of Spring	Ghazanfer Eqbal	76
Spring	P S Christie	77
Spring Is Upon Us	Rajeev Bhargava	78
The Dawning Of Spring	Andrew Smith	79
The Gift Of Spring	Julie Dawe	80
This Is Our Day	Eileen Stuart	81
A Dream Of Spring	Anne S Highman	82
Spring Magic	Alison Ryan	83
April Showers	C J Walls	84
Anode Current	John Allison	85
Gardens	Brain R Russ	86
Awakening	Ted Turl	87
Omens Of The Birds	Valerie Ovais	88
Blissful Spring	Margaret Andrews	89
Blossoming Brilliance	Harriet J Kent	90
Springtime's Serenade	James Leonard Clough	91
Hope Afresh	Clive Cornwall	92
Nature's Gifts	D E Kowalska	93
Spring Rites	Carolyn McDonald	94
Apple Blossom	Kathleen M Hatton	95
The New Beginning	Joiann	96
Roddy	K M Clemo	97
Lakeland Wild Flowers	Alex Branthwaite	98
Nature's Treasures	A Hattersley	99
Singing Worlds	Irene Gunnion	100
Twenty Second Scene	Patricia Holland	101
Dawning Beauty	Sarah Bradley	102
So Near My Heart	D G Hill	103

LITTLE RAGGED ROBIN

His coat is torn
His shoes are worn
Most idle of them all I know
Is little *ragged* robin.
Yet nature touched his head
With gold, and heaven gave his smile
An angel gave his heart to hold.
Joy mostly all the while
His eyes so true - like flowers blue
Oh little ragged robin.
His cheeks so rosy - oh so red.
Covered half *with* jam and bread.
Little ragged robin
You have so little
Yet have so much
The magic touch
Little ragged robin.

Joan Patrickson

WAGTAIL

All through the winter you came around,
When frost and snow bedecked the ground.
You flaunted your coat of black and white,
Not even the gulls put you to flight.
Your companions are sparrows, gardens your home,
Though occasionally down by the river you roam.
No hopping for you, you strut on your feet
You don't have much voice, but then you're petite.
Whatever the weather, come rain or come shine
You run o'er the lawn on insects to dine.
Called the pied wagtail, it couldn't be better,
A name so descriptive fits you to the letter.
How you lighten my day when you come into view!
Oh what joy! You've a mate. Now there are two.

Evelyn Balmain

WAKE, BEAUTIFUL ROSE (A VILLANELLE)

Wake, beautiful rose, from your winter's sleep.
Do not be afraid for springtime is near.
Free those petals from which your blossoms leap.

Display nature's beauty, hidden so deep.
Share with us the secrets that you hold dear.
Wake, beautiful rose, from your winter's sleep.

Let loose those buds before they grow too steep.
Open your heart, there is nothing to fear.
Free those petals from which your blossoms leap.

Those fragrant smells you can no longer keep.
Fill the air again, as you do each year.
Wake, beautiful rose, from your winter's sleep.

Birds and bees wait, for your harvest, to reap.
Those peaches and creams are now almost here.
Free those petals from which your blossoms leap.

Warmed is the earth from which you slowly creep.
The world is ready for you to appear.
Wake, beautiful rose, from your winter's sleep.
Free those petals from which your blossoms leap.

David Barrow

A Garden In Spring

The garden comes to life
after a long dark hibernation
Lazy bees buzz round the newly
formed blossom,
Doing their bit for nature.
Birds steal aubretia from the rockery
to line their new built nests.

Plants that lay dormant through
the bleak winter, burst into bud.
Smiling pansies turn their faces
towards the sun.
Their stalks dancing in the breeze.

Sleepy butterflies trying out their
wings.
Ladybirds set up house among the
privet.
The weak sun filters through their
leafy windows.
Ants make their endless journeys
to only they know where.
Spider spins busily inviting unsuspecting
guests to its lair.
Delicate silver trails left by snails
endeavouring to reach the fence's summit.

All this activity stirs me into motion
Lazily I reach for the spade.

Adrianne Jones

CAPRICIOUS SPRING

The spring is so reliable
Yet at the same time
So unreliable.

I really should explain
That while the sun shines brightly
Soon it is going to rain.

Blooms in abundance on the trees
Are oft swept away
By a chill spring breeze.

So brief their stay, their time so short
Feast your eyes
Before they are caught.

The magnolia glows as twilight descends
Until the frost strikes
And its beauty ends.

Trees everywhere turn a beautiful green
Shades dark and light - even gold
Can be seen.

Wildlife rejoices and all the birds sing
In praise of the joyous
Return of the spring.

Barbara Fosh

THE LONGING

I live in the north of Scotland
Where spring is a reticent thing.
We see pictures on television
And in newspapers, of southern spring.

By the time our tiny snowdrops
Have struggled with genuine snow,
The south has moved onto daffodils
'By the lake, where they're all ablow.'

By the time we've got our daffies,
Blowing their silent trumpets,
The south has deck chairs out for tea,
With cucumber nibbles and crumpets.

By the time our trees are gingerly
Opening the first frond or two,
The south is basking in blossom -
Oh, what on earth can we do?

We can stand and breathe the clean air
And applaud the tenacity and strength
Of the plants that bring us contentment
In a spring of prodigious length!

D M Anderson

BEAUTIFUL SPRING

I see and hear beautiful spring
From somewhere out in the garden
The blackbird sweetly sings
Notes of enchantment from lark and thrush
And the forest flame pieris plant
Is having its springtime flush
Pink cherry blossom along the avenues
Listen for that bird
Who calls out cuckoo, cuckoo, cuckoo
Masses of crocus, lilac, white and gold
Are a gorgeous sight to behold
Woodlands carpeted with bluebells here and there
The dream of spring is everywhere
April showers to quench the flowers
Giving way to sunny gardening hours
Watching sunlight dancing
On the ripples of the stream
Amongst valleys with grass lush green
High upon the top of the fells
There grows wild purple heather
Alert to every signal and command
Shepherd and sheep dog unite working together
Come sunshine hail or storm
Late hillside lambs are being born
What joyful events nature brings
As she unveils her dream of spring.

Joan Taylor

HAPPY REST AMID GLORIOUS VIEW

The sun with its beams so bright and shining
As you sit on your deck chair, relaxed and reclining
The smile on your face is beaming too,
Amid the spring blossoms and glorious view
There is a light breeze and cooling air;
You have done your spring cleaning, you haven't a care!

Marjorie Cowan

FRESH VIBES FOR ALL

The garden's becoming busy
Spring is in the air:
Keep your eyes wide open
There's lots of movement going on out there:
Take real care and keep alert
A change is taking place:
Twittering birds and humming bees
Nests being built in trees:
Colourful blooms and grass luscious green
A wonderful brightness making a glorious scene:

If you haven't got a garden
Or sadly you can't see or hear:
Just being in the open . . .
You'll sense that springtime's here:
The aroma of flowers
The gentle breeze
Nothing will stop you feeling these:
Mother Nature is truly amazing
To all of us - it's totally free.

Julie Powell

Kaleidoscope

Sunny banks of golden hue
Dotted crimson amongst the blue
Lilac blankets covering ground
Honey fields flaying round

Amongst the hedgerows flowers white
Before the berries of darkest night
Thistle ragwort grasses tall
Dance as taffeta at a ball

Greens, a paint box cannot hold
So many . . . shades from time untold
Silver birches, rowans red
Willows gentle swaying heads

Ancient walls of granite grey
Adorned with ivy flowers gay
Rainbow gardens, in villages small
Black-beamed houses, spires tall

Rolling hills and moorland green
Meandering far to be ever seen
Cattle roam where rabbits play
Upon *God's* hills this sunny day

Mystery and magic round every bend
Rolling waters that never end
Musty walls of the castle's keep
Gentle sloping pebbled streets

Tiny villages lost in time
With roses deep as reddest wine
Now my feet stand firmly down
As I gaze slowly round

As a kaleidoscope, ever turning
Changing beauty, peaceful yearnings

Susan Goldsmith

SPRING 1986

You wouldn't think this month was May -
Hardly a leaf in sight,
The weather's like an autumn day,
Our climate isn't right!

Yet birds are building in the trees
'Midst twigs and branches bare,
Their nests are little wooden balls left
Hanging in mid-air!

Spring lambs and calves have all been born
Shelt'ring by clumps of grass
From whistling wind and misty morn,
Hoping this dream will pass . . .

Spring flowers have bloomed and days grown long
 - It's all happened on time -
Our climate must be all confused
Somewhere along the line!

Carolyn Smith

EARTH'S RESURRECTION

A symbol of new life appears,
Forcing its way through the soil like a tiny green spear.
A sign of earth's vigour renewed,
After winter's heavy grey lassitude.

Buds appear on stripped-bare boughs,
Like tiny green beads sprinkled from the fleeting clouds.
A snowdrop - its perfect head bowing,
In reverence to the new life coming.

The first daffodil bursts open,
A symbol of nature's resurrection.
A sign of the earth's promised treasure,
Always too marvellous to measure.

Spring, the season of reassurance,
Of Mother Earth's continued existence.
But remember, do not take her so much for granted,
Treat her well, for one day soon she may become disenchanted!

Linda M Crook

SPLASH OF SPRING COLOUR

Vanguard of spring
Snowdrops swaying with the wind,
Lightening dark earth,
Sudden welcome sighting,
Banishing dullness;
Cloudy sunless
Skies,
Breathe deeply the air
Spring's purest fare,
Breathe deeply the air.
A waterfall
Of pink blossom cascading
Balconies or fence,
A flowered-covered wall,
Clematis daubs countless,
Pink showers of
Blooms,
A spring showpiece;
Awe-inspiring masterpiece.
Rich harlequin colours,
Polyanthus, violets,
Varied hue crowns
Wearing slim-bodiced green gowns,
A canvas of colour
An artist's palette,
Vying one another,
Paint me! Paint me!
Vying one another
Paint me!

Hilary Jill Robson

CAN SPRING BE FAR BEHIND?

Spring - the very word can lift the spirits,
When icy winter holds us in its thrall
With dark nights, gloomy days and biting cold,
Bare trees, dank fields, no colour anywhere!
As the first shoots pierce the barren earth
And hints of sunshine part the heavy clouds,
So despair recedes:
Winter loosens its cruel grip
As snowdrops appear, braving the elements,
Promising renewal.
Soon colours abound -
Bright yellow, deepest blue and pastel pink,
Fresh varied shades of green;
The air is filled with birdsong,
The sound of lambs and bees.
Life, colour, warmth abound
Proving that solace follows grief.
    Spring is the epitome of hope -
        The return of Persephone!

E M Spencer

STIRRING OF HOPE

I love it when the blackthorn blows
on the sleeping trough of winter.
It cheers the spirit's weariness
to see the crest of early spring
washing the senses with hope.
We may wait long for nature's bounty
the bright brave blooms -
these early flowers kindling hope
enough to soothe the weary.

Joan R Gilmour

SPRING

Skeleton branches creeping to the sky, 'neath a ceiling of azure blue,
are waiting to be dressed in their summer gowns of multi-green shades and hues.
Only the sound of cooing doves is the overture of the scene,
of spring with its golden colours, replacing new life where the old has been.

Nothing can stop the bursting forsythia's gold display on the cottage wall.
Primroses bloom in the woodlands, where beech and ash stand so tall.
The wren the blackbird and robin, look for a place to make their nest,
The squirrel, the hedgehog and others, wake up from their winter's rest.

The closing scene of winter, sees the peeping shoots of the rose.
Along the drive to the big house, a row of snowdrops pose.
Then after the crocus have faded, standing alert in the wing
Daffodil's gold trumpets, herald the chorus of spring.

Geoffrey Ackroyd

A Dream Of Spring

Waking in the morning to sunlight crashing through drawn curtains
Greedy baby birds, their open beaks bigger than their bodies
Send their parents out tugging at hard-working worms

Green buds peak boldly through the soil
Weeds surge up, towering over hibernating gardeners
Hedges abandon shape, reaching out inquisitively to trip up paths

Buildings recently bent in winter gloom
Stretch tall and proud toward the sun
Their concrete walls sparkle and glitter, seeming to dance

Easter emits flock south, choking roads and beaches
Parking, free and deserted in winter, is raced for and paid for
And the weather measured by takings in the tourist trade

The central heating is turned off
Husbands burst with DIY enthusiasm
Venturing outdoors, armed with brushes and paint

Kittens chase flies and web-spinning spiders
Older cats stretch out sleepily in sunny corners
Watching birds lazily, as they boldly pass by

Housewives are out hanging up washing
Their bent backs burnt by early sunshine
Turning tedious chore into leisurely pleasure

Then torrential rain and sudden cold weather
Abandon us all in winter gloom
Booking brochure holidays in sunny Spain

But a few days later the sun wins through
The trees and grass bursting with green
Spring is restored, our moods are too.

T Harris

SEASONS CHANGE

As I sit in cottage comfort
rake the fire and toast my feet.
I think ahead to blue skied April.
Lambing. Cowslips. Shifting sheep.
I'm cosy with winter but I wait for spring.

I like to see the buds on hedgerows.
Blooms in gardens gathered in.
Pretty arrangements adorning alcoves.
People give their lawns a trim.

Now I'm older I listen to each chime of the clock.
Seasons change so quickly.
I wish time would halt the tide.

Joan M Emmens

SPRINGTIME

Now Spring has spread her mantle gown of green,
And daffodils add to the beauteous scene.
With crocuses and tulips dotted gloriously around,
The birds that are returning, making such a joyous sound.
Gardens looking green once more,
Spring is here so clean and pure.
Though March winds blow, and April showers,
Threaten to ruin all the flowers.
To see the birds upon the wing
It's such a joy to welcome spring.
When rain is getting warmer, lambs gambol in the fields
Fine shrubs giving out a gorgeous blossom yield.
Rainbows appear through sun and falling rain,
Of one thing I am certain, Spring is here again.

Eileen Burton

NEW BEGINNINGS

the christmas lights have been tucked away
greeting cards from the shelves long gone
an easter bunny scurried passed today
the transition to spring has begun

the dark nights are giving way to the light
feathered friends sing in sweet harmony
you feel sure your future can only be bright
when such beauty is given for free

the hillsides are dotted with daffodils wild
gracefully they dance in the breeze
on a carpet of green, bluebells stand with pride
while crocuses cosset the trees

a mother duck passes swimming proudly in the lake
her siblings in formation close behind
their velvet-textured feathers they flutter and shake
as between the scrawny reeds they twist and wind

new-born lambs in the fields can be seen
encircling their mother as they play
they skip and run in the grass so green
never wandering too far away

lovers they stroll in the afternoon sun
their enthusiasm knows no bounds
although inevitable this season would come
how the beauty of spring still astounds

Shirley Ann Lewis

SPRING

Small children gaze happily
At fluffy new-born lambs
Taking their first slow tentative steps
In a yellow sea of daffodils.
Elderly people admire
The crisp, deep, intense blue
Of the sky
And take in the beautiful greenery
As they close their eyes
And picture memories
From long ago.
Tiny, lush, green buds
Wet and glistening
From the morning dew
Blossom into breathtaking shades
Of picturesque flowers.
Everybody, everywhere,
Stops and smiles
Looking up at the sky
In perfect unison
As the first bud of spring
Opens itself up to the world
And they realise
A new year, a fresh start.

Becky Robinson (13)

LOOKING FORWARD

Surprise is the essence of life
It lifts us up into the realms of hope
There is no end to its scope
We can call this emotion kind
For some, gives the chance to unwind
And when the day is dull
We feel that pull
Of ambitious scenes
And avenues to travel
Till it warms the air
Keeps away despair.
Maybe this is part fantasy
Which grows and grows
Keeps us on our toes.
Yes! This is spring!
Our hearts unite to sing,
A wonderful surprise each year
When primroses and daffodils appear
As if none had gone before
A wonderful world
For us to explore.

Joan Hands

WHAT SPRING INSPIRES

Amidst all that is confusing in this life,
Through all that is sorrow and of joy
The season stands as rocks along a shore
That guides us to the harbour of our voyage.

Spring is the light and an end to strife,
An end to winter's rage, that seems so void.
No longer do we hide beyond our walls
And close our eyes against the season's ply.

Spring is the joy to which we seek in life
When heavy hearts then rise and strife aside
We welcome home the beauty we recall,
Of summer, before the birds in flock did fly

To warmer days abroad and to longer light
All of nature's land will bloom beneath the sky,
Flocks now home from the land of foreign shores
They build again the nests where chicks will lie

Until the day when grown they take to flight
Every creature seeks a mate with eager eyes
For spring is here and chance must be to lure
For the species to uphold if they should die.

Each day we gather strength from such delight
With the early morn when the sun begins to rise
And promises the joy of a long winter's cure
For the air we breathe is scented with new life.

Our hearts' desires will chance that distant sight
And doubts will cease our hearts to agonise,
Over things we cannot change or know for sure
Then far reaching, we find what spring inspires.

Karen Bailey

SPRINGTIME

Pink cherry blossom petals,
Like snowflakes on the grass,
The morning dew on bushes,
Like silver beads of glass,
The early morning birdsong,
With its joyful ring,
All telling me the glorious news:
It's spring, it's spring, it's spring!

Snowdrops and crocus blossoms,
Their time already past.
Now daffodils and tulips
Parading proud at last.
The golden warming sunrays
Life's new forces bring.
The bursting buds on bushes shout:
It's spring, it's spring, it's spring!

Helga I Dharmpaul

SUNNY DAYS

Semi-naked bodies,
basking in the sun.
Little children splashing,
games are lost and won.
Mothers watching children,
Fathers watching Mum.
Semi-naked bodies,
basking in the sun.

Anna King

Preceding Spring

Winter still gripped us in its cruel grey fingers,
A north wind roared across the fields.
Hands in pockets and heads tucked down
We trudged through the mud, far away from the town
'Til we came to the top of the hill.
A copse formed a crown at the summit,
Bare treetops beckoned us inside,
But as we stepped in there was silence,
Sudden silence from the fury outside.

A miracle had happened in that small winter wood,
A scene I'll remember 'til I die.
There on that cold, bleak, dreary winter's day
Hearts lifted in wonder, we gazed at the display;
Covering the ground beneath those leafless trees
As far as the eye could see
Spread the delicate lace of white anemones -
Lighting up the day; lighting from below the waiting wood,
And lightening our lives in that moment of delight, so unexpectedly.

Joan Page

BLOSSOM TREE

There's a blossom tree at the bottom of our garden,
With so very soft-white clouds of velvet blooms,
And perched upon the highest branch is a wood pigeon,
Singing beautifully and tending to his plumes.

I sit and watch the branches swaying freely,
As the cool spring breeze goes rushing through the tree,
I wish that it would never change appearance,
But the blossoms will be back this time next year.

Jane Smith

Spring Song

Tiny, thin, thrifty leaves leap forth, from mother's cold, damp, dank earth they came
Unfurling, uncurling in unison, unabashed exhibiting beautiful spring-line shades:
Smooth silvery-green, mint, emerald, new-born baby yellow
Long, tall, flat, round shapes, stealthy, steaming, congregating - weaving webs
After the long winter went to sleep - after many days, many days
Nature chorus and herbs herald the coming spring

Timely as the hour hand on a clock face they grow
Gay flowers, budding, blooming, attributes array stands out
Kiss by the breeze, they give off wonderful scent:
Cowslips, bluebells and pretty golden flower-head of Alexandras
Reach for the sunny morning country climes
Emerging primroses and sweet violets relishing spring
Graciously offering their treasures, a salutation of new life to the world

Breath of spring alight through hazel catkins on parade
Tiny flowers dust the cool, biting air with pollen - spring's song
Hand in hand, in sweet repose dancing on a carpeted tapestry
Of aromatic shades of green, mellow yellow courting - good companions
Harvesting their precious gifts along graceful pathways from their perfume beds

Rosetta Stone

SPRINGTIME

Spring is here and the flowers grow
Birds are resting in the hedgerow.
There's smiles on the faces of people you see
Everyone's happy as bright as can be.
The reason why, is spring is here
Everyone's full of good health and cheer.
It's funny to think how it changes your mood
Once you felt sad but now you are shrewd.
You start thinking of things up ahead
Like where shall I plant my new flower beds?
Spring cleaning the house is no trouble at all
Everything's shining including the hall.
The windows let in God's heavenly light
Shining on crystal they look ever so bright.
Isn't it great you feel so alive
Only last month you thought you would not survive,
I'm feeling great, isn't it fine?
Oh how I love spring I think it's devine.

May Kay

HEAVEN'S COUNTRY

As winter sought hibernation
The sunlight escapes
I walk from the dark into spring's wondrous regime
Her colours invite you without the problems of words
It's like waking from sleep into a beautiful dream

Spring soothes the belief of the sabbatical hearts
Happiness circulates in the pardon we lease
Free of the oppression of the long winter's nights
We are adopted by the season of peace

Fields compromise with daffodils
Gardens submit to the rose
Tulips sanction an invasion into the heart of romance
The days shine with affection smiles rain with pride
Upon tapestries of innocence where young lambs may dance

Dawn blossoms each morning and perfumes the day
Spring carries the fragrance on a warm friendly breeze
As rivers seize independence in a sociable coup
Streams ripple their pleasure through harmonious trees

I enter the moment
To experience the mood
Watching the anatomy of nature in a picturesque truce
They all flock together in a fashionable siege
Like an annual reunion with a seasonal excuse

This rebirth of a poem this renaissance with love
Can be heard on the day nature sings
As I follow the chorus into the memory of May
I walk heaven's country with the permission of spring

David Bridgewater

RECOLLECTION

Hot and humid as we stand.
Looking at, 'The Tokens of Remembrance'.
The grass is neatly cut
and fir trees line a border to the right, standing proud and erect.
Neatly below them are a quantity of headstones.
Some white marble, others black, shining in the summer sun.
A son on his hands and knees tidies his father's grave,
bending on the ground, his concentration sound.
A beautiful cool breeze blows right through us,
as he stands, wiping his hands.
On the side is a wooden bench a resting place,
surrounded by dozens of wild bluebells carpeting the ground.
Loud peals of bell ringing can be heard from the church.
The garden is covered in splendour with many coloured daffodils,
soaking in the summer heat.
We stand in the shade of an old oak tree.
The wind embraces us with the saints of old,
looking after their own
as we climb up
and make our way home.

Pat Jones

Conscious Threshold

Every conscious reflection
On life's constant nowness
Is another new spring:
Spring as life regeneration, as
Birth of all things pure,
Of utmost beauty and perfection,
As the aiming of a dart of dreams
That knows its true, full potential
To reach the summit of a full life
Lived,
To realise man's highest, purest, most
Swollen and soaring dreams.
Every minute, if reflected on, is
Spring beginning,
Is the threshold of nurturing life itself
From smallest, most fragile seed
To fullest, most sweet and strong and beautiful
Tree. A tree is reality, but so can a dream be!
How easy, what convenient temptation
To believe life is fullest in winter
When the cycle is complete . . .
But wait! . . . cycles revolve
And one revolution is never sufficient . . .
As the wheel turns it becomes
Smoother, faster, more svelte and perfected.
Be ready always and pushing for the next revolution,
The next start, new growth, with resolve and high ideals . . .
The next spring is always now
If you so want it to be.

Gemma Parkes

SPRING HAS SPRUNG

Spring to me is the invisible artist.
The true provider of colour.
Every garden, field and plain
Is a canvas.
With every stroke, something new grows.
Every tree in suitable pose.
From my window I see a willow so supple.
Birds from first light, begin to sing and couple.
Spring a time to welcome new life to the fold.
Spring meaning 'beginning'
A past future will unfold.
Just imagine the noise
If every bluebell could ring,
To herald the arrival of yet another spring.

Derrick Evers

A Meal- Shared

Such commuting from nest to birdtable,
Speckled thrushes quickly spied the repast
Of dried crumbs piled under the little roof
Of bird-feeder and flew down fast!

Beaks bob-bobbing, throats gulping,
Such exultation and chirping over their find,
In eagerness, titbits falling to the path,
Then bills laden, away to offspring left behind.

Witness Nature's spectacle of survival under way!
For some time, back and forth they scurry.
Such a meal laid out for their delight,
To transport it they must hurry.

Banquet finally devoured, they disappear,
Filled and satisfied for the day,
Forgetting the scraps scattered in haste,
No longer hungry, they're away!

To white-collared, grey-morning suited pigeons
A great service they have rendered.
Much too fat to bend under wooden roof,
Beady eyes feast on scraps tendered!

Strutting boldly up the garden path,
They stalk the tasty morsels left behind.
No bother now to peck at remnants
Scattered by departed thrushes - how kind!

Pat Heppel

PORTRAITS IN LACE

The spring-soft mist in spiralling wisps
Will usher each morning, refreshing and crisp
With spangles of sunlight like gold, shining thread
Which naturally nurture each delicate head
Of primrose, or cowslip, or celandine bright,
Of bluebell, and crocus and buttercup light.
The prettiest blossoms can float on the breeze,
Leaving their havens, high up in the trees.
Spring time holds promise like intricate lace
Whose delicate patterns weave portraits of grace:
All we need to do in this season of hope
Is to grow in the lace, not stagnate in rough rope!

Emma Louise Taylor

THE FIVE SENSES OF SPRING

Oh the sweet smell of those rainy woodlands
basking in the yellow sunlight,
whose leaves glisten and whisper my name,
as I wander through the bushes and trees.

Ah, the sight of a baby spring lamb,
jumping over to its mother
for yet another taste of tender milk,
its life only just beginning.

The sound of the waves crashing against the shoreline
bringing fresh, soft, revitalising waters
to soothe away the aches and pains from my feet
as I paddle and wade.

The touch of the most delicate flower
as it begins its furtive life,
awaiting for pollination and the chance
to live again.

Oh! The taste of new potatoes dripping in butter,
salad days that stretch out before me.
Fresh, wholesome foods, now in season.
Oh! Spring is my favourite time of the year!

Susan Skye

Wonderful Spring!

People smile and pass the time of day.
The noise of giggling children at play,
Trees budding, their shades of green,
Flowers, blossoms, in magical scene.

Sweet fragrance of blooms to thrill us,
Returning birds join the dawn chorus.
Longer days, yearned for lighter nights;
Springtime, nature's season of delights.

Again we hear the lawnmowers' sound,
Familiar smell of newly-mown ground.
Young lovers meandering hand-in-hand.
We look forward to holidays, sea, sand.

Our spirits are lifted and hopes renewed.
Healthy outdoor pastimes can be pursued.
We wake early, in harmony with the larks,
Making plans for outings, visiting parks.

Invigorated after the cold season of rest,
Warm breezes of Springtime at her best,
Spur us into action, freed from captivity,
As if all ignited by a surge of electricity.

Homemaking, painting, cleaning done,
Ready for balmy days of summer sun.
A sense of anticipation; it's so exciting,
As we thank God for Wonderful Spring.

Janet Hewitt

FRESH SAP SURGING

Fresh sap surging, urgently swift
As the dead earth yields the fruit of its womb,
And the chill air warms with a breath from the south,
Sends the snowdrop's pale bell as the season's first gift
When life beyond death bursts forth from the tomb,
While May blossom decks that thorn-twisted crown.

Quiet birds wake with pale winter's end
And their stiff throats tune to a new, sweeter key,
Till the pale dawn echoes to sound of their song,
While the old steeple sways with the bells as they ring
In the joy of a dawn from the darkness set free
By the surge of that Life no death can deny.

New life blooms in pasture and wood
As a heartbeat that quickens to spring's urgent plea,
And young lambs leap where the meadows are green,
And the young birds peep, while wild hares bound,
While the blood of the Lamb, and the shade of the tree
Brings the light of the Son, and the sunlight of love.

M Scroggs

SMELLS LIKE SPRING

What can I smell
What's that? What's that?
Asks the farmer in his hat
That smells good
What is it? What is it?
Asks the sparrow in a flying visit
Ask the field mouse, squirrel or hare
You could even ask the grumpy old bear
And they'll surely know without a doubt
What the fuss is all about
For as they awake and get out of bed
We will all go and ask them what lies ahead
And then they will tell us
As the birds start to sing
We are all waking up
To celebrate spring.

Louise C Fletcher

THE GIFT OF EASTER

A special time of year
A new beginning - all is fresh and new
New life re-awakens
A new season has begun.

When nature casts her magic wand
And blossom and leaf in harmony bond,
New formations soon discovered
New growth - once dormant - now recovered.

In woodlands where the soil is nourished
With compost of autumn's decay,
A new growth appears that covers the ground,
Where early primroses are found.

This lovely season brings the perfume of spring flowers,
Sustained by early morning dew, and gentle April showers.
Sunbeams filter through the trees - descending low,
And blankets the earth with an iridescent glow.

Matched by leaves unfurling to spread a golden sheen,
These tiny flowers raise their heads in shades of yellow and cream.
Is this all a master plan that measures every season,
Or is this all by chance - a dowry with no reason?

Joy M Jordan

FEBRUARY 14TH

Stout, successful bumblebees
Are clambering on top of the crocus flowers;
Collared doves (blue collar, white collar, even jobless?)
Are mate-chasing in the naked tree;
The swept and symmetrical slabs
Are confounded by shocks of virgin primroses
Coming up smiling all over the place
In the warmest February anyone has ever remembered.
The warmest I remember, anyway,
Because your gut-red card struts its stuff on my desk
Bellowing the hot-air of hope.

Daphne Rance

SEE, SMELL AND LISTEN TO SPRING

See, smell and listen to spring
Look and see what spring will bring
Butterflies and bumblebees
All sorts of insects just like these

Look and see, open your eyes
The winter has gone now
But spring has arrived

Open your mind take notice of this
You can see things which you might have missed
Don't be blind open your mind
Spring is for each and every kind
There's all sorts of things which you ought to see
Take a look just like me
There's birds building nests
Frogs are spawning

Wake up open your eyes spring is dawning

Open your ears and take in the sounds
There's blackbirds singing
And the hares stomping ground

So just stop a moment take time to listen
Look on the ground the dewdrops glisten
Can you smell the fragrance of spring?
And to each new dawn a new day will bring
Now that you have seen, smelled and listened to spring

Elizabeth (Burke) Mayes

ALMOND BLOSSOM

Sweet almond blossom harbinger of spring
Thus scores of readers doubtless will rehearse
And naught is left for me to sing
Who fain would earn a pittance by my verse
Pink almond blossom when the trees are bare
Gladly we welcome your sweet bloom again
Like precious stones most valued and most rare
Thus one and all will write in varied strains

So would I echo all their songs of praise
So parrot like my feeble tribute bring
To beauty that brings cheer in lengthening days
Sweet almond blossom harbinger of spring
Nothing is new the wise men said of old
Yet still new joy the changing seasons bring
And now the least as many a pen has told
Is almond blossom herald of the spring.

R D Hiscoke

BEAUTIFUL SPRING

The spring is here at last
Making the plants breed exceedingly fast
Giving them delight every day
Oh! In a wonderful desirable way

The trees are waking to brighten the dawn
Popping out leaves to adorn the lawn
Spreading their branches to make a great show
Giving flower dancers a brilliant glow

Animals awaking to greet the new day
Laughing and screeching in their animal way
Thinking of loving each other so much
Even desiring the creative touch

Birds of every description we know
Are chirping with considerable delight
Spring's new creations are happy and bright
Singing in chorus not wishing to fight

Insects do the tango at every occasion
Flapping their wings to the tune in confusion
Greeting their friends in a spring like manner
Hoping these friends will like them sing Hosanna!

The spring brings to life Mother Earth herself
She scatters her abundance of mineral wealth
Making sure her work is well done
And visibly glows when seeing the sun.

Alma Montgomery Frank

BEAUTIFUL SPRING!

Trumpeting daffodils play out a tune,
An exuberant release from harsh winter gloom.
Sweet scented mahonia, in her last flush of flower,
Attracts the first butterfly, in the midday hour.
Savouring the taste of nectar within,
Quietly basking with warmth on her wing.
Anemone blanda of white, pink, and blue
Open their eyes when the sun shines through,
And whisper to crocus who tell of their dreams,
Giggling together with dry rustling leaves,
That run round in circles, at a slight breath of air,
Clicking their heels to the branches bare.
A pretty blue pansy with a small cheeky face,
Gives a look of pure charm and elegant grace
To the miniature narcissi, silk petals of cream,
A love affair imminent, can clearly be seen.
Melodious songs, from the brave hearted wrens,
An encore requested for the performance again,
To welcome this day and all that is new,
Friends of the garden will always stay true.

Jane Rennie

SAD

To seeping cold I did succumb.
A winter, oh far too dreary.
Although darkness now withers
My spirit just dithers
The prospects seem so bleary.

Quite suddenly the sun comes forth
And spring is here again.
The twigs thicken with buds of green.
I, with winter do remain.

Flowers after vernal equinox
Cause me to pause, to pull up my socks.
Bluebells and sprigs of golden gorse,
Steer me to a happier course;
And take away the pain.
My heart is young again.

Dennis Walker

Joy

To see the sunrise in the morning,
hear the dawn chorus great each new day
feel the wind in my hair,
the warmth of the sun
and the cooling rain on my face.

Watch a mystical coloured rainbow
as it reaches across the sky,
greet dusk with a beautiful red sunset,
see the stars brightly twinkle at night,
as the man in the moon smiles widely
and dances around his heaven in delight.

To listen to the music of thunder,
crashing its symbols and drums,
see lightning reaching out its fingers
trying to touch everything and everyone.

To hear the sound of laughter,
a voice says 'Hello' and 'I miss you,'
a smile and a hug and to know I am loved
by the people I love
these are the best things in this world to me

Gez Larkin

SPRING

There's a smell of fresh cut grass,
When spring is in the air.
The sound of birds singing,
Tending their nest with care.

Buds are in abundance on the trees,
When spring is all around.
Yellow fields of daffodils disappear
As wallflowers and tulips fill the ground.

The seasons are changing,
When spring begins to fade.
Profusion of multi-coloured primroses,
Catching the eye throughout the day.

Ida Dunwoodie

SPRING, MARCH 1999

The sky is light and luminous,
The air is soft,
Faraway the warplanes roar.
Who will end the crying?
He moves unknown among the sick,
Waiting to bring the world,
Eternal spring.

U Johnson

NOTICING SPRING

Waking in spring when sun is shining
Back to the world in all breathing
It is time to feel the morning
Its sight, its touch need no adorning.
I, April set the bittersweet task
But living the sun, no need to ask,
When born could say 'Mother, give me the sun'
The season on face! Don't leap to the one.

Above, the blue and the gold
Senses sharp, can still feel cold
There is no need for detail stale
But will writhe, and then will fail.
Winter's passed, my love, leave the loose sweater!
Days of the sun when I first met her.
Now jumping, spinning in the rapture
A blind control of the capture.

The sky is blue, a dark heavy blue
The rain could easily fall anew.
Kids play out late, evening shouts across the street
Her and I, we should meet.
Lower, the sky is red, nearer the horizon
Enthralment, the breeze, and an explanation.
This picture breathed over and over again
And oh to dig up the riches from then.

Edmund Humphreys

'Passion' - Ate?

Seductively she danced before him
And he advanced his eyes adoring
She'd set his passionate pulses racing
With promises of their embracing . . .

He watched her as she pirouetted
Her hour-glass figure silhouetted
Against translucent lacy netting
For her, a perfect boudoir setting.

They danced together both gyrating
Pausing, straddling copulating
Her body language of emotion
Convincing him of her devotion . . .

He'd wooed her, loved her and they'd mated
And then, completely satiated
He happily lay down beside her
And . . . she ate him that black widow spider!

Dulcie Levene

BEARER OF THE SPERM

Winter's cool yet coddled comfort
Precedes claustrophobic days.
A pause within the cycle
While Spring and Winter plays -
out their yearly tug-o-war
'Twix cold and surging heat.
Summer looms so heavily,
'Til Winter's truly beat.
Spring bounces back, then forward,
Life surges through her veins.
Blessed host of mundane sperm
Rejoices through her pains.
Labours-on, complete renewal,
Then Summer steals the scene.
Forward still to Winter
As she goes, so has she been.
True Almighty Magic,
A fairytale foretold.
Creates - uncertain future
Destroying the days of old.

Shirley Sammout

THE CELANDINE

Look into my golden cup and see eternal hope,
for I spring from the earth smiling each year without fail,
brought to life by the soft touch of Mother Nature's gentle fingers.
I bring you joy as you gaze upon my beauty
and I flower for you, just you
as taking your daily walk you talk to me
so I grow strong within your love.
Every day you come to see if I still bloom
and always I am here to greet you with my cup of gold
full beyond compare with the richness of life
and it's all for you, just you.
But I grow weary as the year grows old
and weep as I leave you to sleep my long sleep,
but next spring I will once more greet you with my cup of gold
and your heart will lift again when the year is young.

Paddy Jupp

SPRING

Spring is here, oh such pleasure,
Long golden days for us to treasure.
A time of renewal for trees and flowers,
Hopefully sunshine and refreshing showers.

The birds sing their songs oh so sweet,
We go for beautiful walks, oh such a treat.
Through lush green fields, the wildlife all around,
We savour it all, such joy to be found.

The daffodils nod in the morning breeze,
The buds burst and open on the trees.
Such beauty there is if we only look,
With summer to follow and new hopes afoot.

Barbara Ann Barker

YESTERDAY'S PIZZA

In this odd society
Sometimes I have to try,
Not to think too seriously . . .
Better laugh than cry!
I won't get into politics . . .
I won't get into strife . . .
I won't get into antics,
That wield the ethnic knife;
I will not touch on leaders
Who seem so out of touch,
And start things based on counsellors,
Whose vision wants for much!
I'm thinking of another side
Of the world we're living in,
That saner people try to hide,
Bearing it within a grin;
We're in a world of 'fairness'
Where all must have a chance,
Such as the kind of offices,
Lead everyone a dance!
Intermingling services,
Gas and electricity,
Airlines, trains and buses,
And social commentary;
It may suit adolescents,
Their adulthood almost found;
But those who've been around awhile . . .
Are not sure of their ground!

Tom Ritchie

SOS On Earth

Planet earth is our home,
it doesn't belong to us alone.
God made it for the insects, birds and the bees,
the animals, mammals and the trees.

It's the only place,
where we can all survive.
If we don't do something soon,
we won't be alive.

Pollution from buses,
lorries and cars
will leave our planet,
resembling Mars.

Pollution from factories,
that runs into streams.
It's hell on earth,
a nightmare in dreams.

The fish that swim,
the oceans and seas
are certainly dying,
because of man's lees.

Threats from broken fridges,
aerosol gases,
nuclear weapons,
and their ashes.

Some people care,
some people don't.
They've been asked to help,
but they won't.

We're going to pay,
the same price in the end.
You've been warned,
goodbye, my friend!

R Glendenning

OUTSIDE IN SPRING

What I perceive is how they live
He sings, she plays - they breathe.

Often knowing not how, or why or who
made their abilities beyond their knowledge
                              - Yet so true.

From someone greater than him
and more humble and gracious than her
who mobilated their dance and movement like that.

No stopping would prevail
All the riches of this world
Nor disbelief in another - who created the first
Only suffering to a self
Would replace this distrust and melt
All the vision and passion deep inside.

Naomi Elisa Price

THE CAT AND TOAD WELCOMING PARTY

The cat won't be going to London,
When her mistress moves house. The buyer
Will have to love pussies; and toads, too.
Some deal to accustom oneself to,
The specification's no liar!

Both creatures will have to be cared for.
The garden pond mustn't run too dry,
Or toads will decide to play changeling
And not lay their spawn here next spring.
for its good, nature can be so sly.

Sons would love to take jamjars of them
To teachers, for class nature tables,
And watch goggle-eyed, as each tadpole
Tears out of spawn-gel in a fishbowl
And swims as soon as its tail enables.

Gillian Fisher

SPRINGTIME

Spring is the best time,
The Earth awakes after the cold, dark sleep
Of winter and the warm sun stirs new life into being.
The first of many flowers open their petals
To await the first solitary brave bee.
He brings a promise of sweeter joys to come.
A hesitant, early butterfly reminds us of warmer days ahead.
All is new and fresh,
New life, from the old, has begun once more.
My life has begun again,
I have left behind my winter of bitter tears and dark
Weary pain; for I have awakened to find my loved ones at my side.
So do not grieve; instead remember I am but a thought away,
Gone, forever, is my old life.
I am reborn - into a new life of endless days,
Full of sweetness and warmth,
Be happy, for I am at the start of another spring
And I know the best time is yet to come.

Margaret Poole

A Dream Of Spring!

The golden sun is glistening brightly in the sky.
Cheerful birds sing their beautiful rhymes.
The beaming, bright colours are transforming all around,
Suddenly the crying cold can't be found.
Flowers are opening their petals out wide,
Buzzing bumblebees are attracted to the sparkling look
of the petals which they try to find.
Playful squirrels run around in pairs,
While the twinkling breeze twirls around softly in the fresh air.
Children usually let out a smile, when they see a bright rainbow
high up in the sky.
The darkness does not appear in the fascinating sight,
Everything around seems to glow because of the light.
Most people admire the wonderful moments of life,
When the leaves change colour as the year passes by.

> *I dream of a glorious spring day*
> *and I wish to be a part of it!*

Rebecca Henley

STIRLING HARBOUR BY NIGHT

The sea winds gently teased our ruby-tinged faces after
the long climb upwards, as the sky silently hummed a gentle
orange amber serenade. Our eyes were set adrift on the
splendour of Stirling Harbour twinkling beneath us in all its glory.

We scaled the fence, meant to contain us, and had a bow
seat on our very own tall ship as we glided calmly towards docking.
The house lights sparkled like a shoal of tiny, silver minnows
flitting in the cool evening calm; and beyond them, just darkness.
That was our coastline where land stopped and endless dark
dreamy ocean sprawled infinitely onwards; rolling, swaying
and carrying.

In the distance, a bright lighthouse warned of rocks and hard
endings as we navigated by the stars, numerous as the shimmering
silver-lipped ripples below. The tides lapped up against the small
vessels like a devoted mother to its newborn pup; wetting,
caressing, back and fro, high and low.

It was so peaceful looking down on the harbour, that feeling her
arm delicately tighten around my waist, I remembered that we must
go and set sail on our own special ship another dusk. The sun,
disappearing, kissed the nape of the harbour's neck as gentle
purple and grey-blues echoed from the water's edge and coolness
sank into us as a shiver passed unnoticed.

Martin Boddie

Something New!

How can I say something new
That's not been said before?
Darling! Je t'adore?
That's become a bore!

Show originality
Find something fresh to say
Instead of just the usual cliché!

You must be fed up with always hearing the same line
'Honey you're divine!'
'Kisses sweet as wine!'

I'm determined to declare my love in a new way,
If only I find something new to say!

But it's not as easy as it might appear
To find a new, *original* idea!
When I get a notion; try to coin a phrase,
Every time I'm back in the old ways!

'Darling I'll be always true!' and
'Dearest I love you!'
'Start our lives anew!'
'Under skies of blue!'

It seems quite impossible to swim against the tide.
I give up! But then, at least I tried!

Geoff O'Neil

SPIRIT OF THE MAY

This haunting,
This subtle stirring of the senses,
Comes,
In balmy stillness,
After sudden rain and sudden sun
And everywhere,
Everywhere, the scent of hawthorn in the air.

Catherine Reay

DARK татоTo Light

Spring from dark to light,
From despair to hope,
Into a wonderful, fresh, new world.
The sky is noisy, full of the chorus of the birds, the low hum
Of the plane and the sound of the not too distant summer.

There is an air of expectancy - full of rebirth and new
Beginnings. Spring is here and the smell is light and flowery,
Pungent with newly-found intoxicating aromas and alive with
Warm, bright colours. The flowers have begun to bloom and the
Grass is becoming lush and overgrown, as we move
From dark to light,
From despair to hope.

And the sky is blue, symbolising creation and in turn
creating happiness,
We walk through a blossom storm and feel the softness on our
Cheeks and the lightness in our footsteps.
The world is forever changing, we are forever changing
From dark to light,
From despair to hope.

The heat from the sun is easy and welcoming, colours everywhere
Sparkle, encapsulated by the new brightness.
The trees sway in time with the new harmony, their leaves rich
With life and colour, their branches full of life, stand strong.
People walk; their heads held high, their eyes sparkling and a
Wide beam across their face. They feel the drift
From dark to light
From despair to hope.

Joanne Clarke

Untitled

There's a new fresh smell in the air
People are shedding the gloom and starting to care
The sky is getting lighter and clearer
Bright sunny days are nearer
Everyone loves to see newborn lambs this season brings
There's a pleasure in wakening to hear the birds sing
The world outside looks like a beautiful picture
No longer are doctors pestered for cold and cough mixtures
People want to go out for walks
They come out of their long silence and start to talk
New flowers have blossomed, trees no longer bare
It's a beautiful new beginning
Spring fills our air.

Kathleen Reid

Promise Of Spring

You walk along a country road
Where trees are heavy with their load
Of tight green buds which seem to say
'Cheer up, spring is on its way.'
The birds are busy all day long
Filling the air with chirp and song
Snowdrops and crocus make a start
Of days to come that will impart
The beauty of tulip and daffodil
The new, fresh, green of vale and hill
Springtime always seems to be
The loveliest time of year to me.

Nan Ogg

PETALS

When rowan blossom
is a cascade of moon flowers
on a warm June night.

When chestnuts hold
their candles high
to set the month of May alight.

When sycamores shed
velvet flowers
down to the earth below.

And May blossom
lightens the hedgerows
snow stars of joy to bestow.

When Queen Anne's lace
garlands ribbon roads
down to the timeless sea,

And poppies startle
the hedgerows
then rejoice and be glad with me.

Margaret Leigh

SPRING DAYS

Deep caverns
Blue waters
Towering trees
Beds of bluebells
And poetry
Spoken by you
Softly encouraging
My youth to share
Your discoveries
Of beauty
As I lay
Looking at skies
Beyond high branches
Glancing at you
Listening to you
From the forest's floor
Of fronds and primroses
Hyacinths and wild daffodils:
The furnishings
Of spring.

Rowland Ablett

POLAROID

The sun arose on a spring morning clear
And greeted me with its delightful kiss;
The day appearing beckon'd me come near
And bid me capture something of its bliss.
Alas I had no canvas, brush nor oil
With which to make a record of that view
But I resolv'd to struggle and to toil
Until a method show'd itself anew.
I labour'd till the sun was going down
But no ideas of mine were bearing fruit;
So hopp'd I on the 95 to town
And bought a camera from a man in Boots.
      No wonder that so many are employ'd
      At the gay pastime of the Polaroid.

Chris Blackmore

SPRINGTIME MELODY

There's such an air of magic around us,
Nature's paintbrush is busy again,
Gone, are the dark days of winter
Replaced by the soft greens of spring.
The bright yellow forsythia is flowering,
Golden daffodils, crocuses in bloom,
Primroses and sweet-smelling violets,
Goodbye to the days of gloom.
Young lambs, dancing, in fields full of daisies,
The countryside wakes from its long winter's sleep,
From somewhere on high the song thrush is singing
Along with the robin and blackbird so sleek.
Once more attired in their bridal gowns,
In shades of soft pink and white,
The trees are crowned in an ethereal glory,
Aglow in shafts of golden sunlight.
Spring is such a glorious season,
Sunshine, gentle breezes and soft falling rain,
Like the strains of a beautiful melody
Promising, new life again.

Rosemary Remy

ONWARD!

O beauteous midwinter,
Slumbering deeply, as a child,
Dream on, dream on,
Through the watery kiss of the wolfmoon,
Through the season of mistletoe,
And be disturbed not in your warm, soft womb,
For feasting has begun;
Both king and thrall share the fireside warmth
In merry midwinter play;
The snow filled, evergreen forests
Resound with their songs,
Songs of rebirth,
Renewal,

For, my beauteous midwinter,
Even as you sleep, dream,
Your sons and daughters of the spring
Have been born!

Seán Rooney

TO PEG, WHO DIED ON 20TH JUNE 1996

Spring will not be spring, nor summer, summer,
Without your fingers imprimatur
Upon the wayside blossoms in their nest
Below the hedge: you always loved the wildings best,
The primrose and the chance sown daffodil,
More than these trumpeting petunias, loud and shrill,
Whose fanfare from this ornamental urn
Is more in tune perhaps, with this year's blowsy June.

For this is where we sat in deckchair weather,
Just you and I, and here we dreamed together
Of an Arcadian world where summer never
Turned to autumn brown - and spring -
Ah spring! Went on forever.

A F L Adams

BLOSSOMS OF THE SPRING

Blossoms of the spring
Flowers of the primrose
Bluebells are here
Spring has come again
Dew is around like one's tear

Blossoms of the hawthorn
And the cherry red and bright
Are reflected by the sunbeam
This shines out golden light

Grass as green and greener
Than I've ever seen before
Carpets of wood once more
Carpet the woodland floor

Spring has come, the blossoms all around
Birds are singing
What a beautiful sound
Thank God I'm living to see this wonder
Blossoms of the spring are here
I smile, I laugh, I dry a tear
For life has been good to me
Spring time is wonderful
Nature's gift I see
Are there to share everywhere
For you and you and me.

A R Williams

I Dream Of Spring

The lovely springtime is the best season of my life!
When the birds sing that lovely melody of spring in every tree in the park and in the garden there is a feast with the little birds in the nests,
And I can't wait for the approach of the summer to enjoy the life,
Splash in hot water of the sea ocean.
That is my best hope, in every spring I come alive again,
But in the cold winter I feel horrible!
But in spring I become a young lover like the birds in the sky,
I like to fly very high with my lover in the sky,
The long days and the lovely warm weather bring out the best of the human interests at his most best,
And also the animals are more alive.
And the gardens and the countryside is all in bloom in green because it is the spring!
What a lovely dream of this wonderful spring!
Give me the springtime and I am the happiest man alive!
I am so happy and so thrilled when approaching the lovely spring!

Antonio Martorelli

A Dream Of Spring

As a pre-teen . . . teen . . .adolescent, adult
I saw spring . . . summer . . . autumn . . . winter
but I did not dream for any one of them
till I reached the final stage of my study in a way
as I console myself
that I have a few more years of education
and after I have completed it
I can dream of spring
in my every moment . . . every day's
kaleidoscopic life's livings
to understand, appreciate and admire
all that I must show patience . . .perseverance
to learn to acquire knowledge
in order to qualify and complete it
that I developed a mental problem
suddenly, instinctively . . . intuitively . . .instantly
I was shattered totally . . . I never recovered
and with it a dream of spring . . . all gone
of I will do this . . . I will do that
I will travel . . . I will write
I will keep in touch of botany . . . finance, fiction writing
hand lines analysis
I will serve every person
as an elected person
to serve all
to be the servant of all

Ghazanfer Eqbal

SPRING

A little miracle today
To tell me spring is on its way
A snowdrop white as white as snow
Just only *God* could make it grow
To give us mortals hope of spring
So praise to god for everything:
The little river running by:
The blueness of a summer sky,
The songs of birds high in the trees,
The coolness of a summer breeze,
In far-off countries there is strife.
They do not know a better life,
The peace of God eludes them all,
They fight regardless lest they fall.

P S Christie

SPRING IS UPON US

The season of life,
hypes up, once again.
Between winter and summer,
vegetation begins.
Budding with greenery,
full-fledged and alive.
Spring is upon us,
renewing its charm.

Rajeev Bhargava

THE DAWNING OF SPRING

She breathed at me
And touched my cheek,
As I turned my front to the wind;
On a glorious dawn
After mighty storms,
I felt her presence near.
She called to me
Her features drifting,
Her morning colours red;
Amidst the field
I had to yield,
And draw her to my ear.
I heard her voice
That whispered roar,
Which spoke of birth and life;
Of summer sun
And midnight fun,
Soon awake once more.
She came to me
Bright eyes still misty,
Her body warming mine;
But will she stay
Just for today,
Or is this the dawning of spring.

Andrew Smith

THE GIFT OF SPRING

Pink are the blossoms on the bough,
Yellow are the daffodils and primroses,
Birds are singing on the wing,
What a lovely day, it's spring.

Our step is much lighter,
We feel so much brighter,
Casting off winter's shadow,
Sun is casting its warmth,
It's spring.

Breathe in this wonderful day,
Wish it could always stay,
Hooray, hooray.
It's spring.

Julie Dawe

THIS IS OUR DAY

Our love came from nowhere,
Fresh as the dawn,
Sweet tender young love,
Happiness to share.

You brought us together, Lord,
Our hearts are knit in thee,
Your way is perfect,
Holy Spirit, guide us all the way.

Christ Jesus, you came once,
To grace a marriage feast,
Grant to us your presence here,
To make our wedding blest.

The sacred vows we made today,
Seal with your love,
And in our union, richly bless,
our hearts in thee made *one*.

Eileen Stuart

A Dream Of Spring

The gales and storms of winter
Just never seem to end:
Battered by the wind and rain
Our weary way we wend.

Noses pressed against the glass,
Watching snowflakes flutter:
Children long to run and splash
In puddles in the gutter.

Sitting by the roaring fire,
Our minds are filled with plans:
We can feel the warmth and light
Of spring's caressing hands.

Goodbye to woolly jumpers,
Farewell to chilblains red:
Welcome shy and bleating lambs,
And all life's joys ahead.

Anne S Highman

Spring Magic

The dark shadow of winter,
Still covers the ground.
Not one bit of colour,
Not one ray of sun.

Silhouetted trees,
Are leafless and dull.
As white heads of snowdrops,
Cautiously appear.

Then suddenly,
From behind the clouds,
Shines the sun - a golden sphere.

The magic of spring,
Gives plants new growth,
And trees their blossom.
While the golden carpet of daffodils,
Sway in the breeze.

The air becomes full of bird song,
And sweet smelling scent,
From hyacinths growing bright and tall.

Everyone is filled with joy and light,
And children dance excitedly,
Like new born lambs,
Playing in the fields.

This is a sure sign,
That spring is here,
Once again.

Alison Ryan (14)

APRIL SHOWERS

Life preparing for new life to begin
The birds are back from their winter's break with their cheerful song at the breaking of dawn and continues all through the day.

The days are longer, so much can be done.
Spring cleaning the house, tidying up the garden, preparing for bar-be-ques and enjoying the garden once again.

Children looking forward to the spring holidays, playing outside with friends which they have made.

Let's not forget Easter beginning with Good Friday, thinking of Christ being crucified upon a tree we call the cross,
For our vary sins.
Easter comes around and the celebrations begin for Christ conquered death by rising from the tomb in which he was laid.

The sky is blue with the sun shining down on the land which is full of wonderful life.
A few April showers fall from the sky to help the land grow and nature to flourish.

C J Walls

ANODE CURRENT

The newt had heard the news
and passed it on.
Frogs croaked it for a while:
Then with a smile the watcher at the bank,
whose lank line long hung limp untended as he brooded,
thoughts from fish and bait far straying,
rose and quietly went his way
through tweedy bent, past swaying tree tops
and a white wool whittled sky
where high curling swifts' parade of falling leaf, chandelle,
betrayed their long foreknowledge.
Blackbird's bell notes chiding roused the lower dwellers
from their artless drowse.
Leaves, grey-bearded green, poised hovering
in the sheen smooth air, made no remark. They Knew!

With delicate tread, as one who takes a loaded tea-tray over stones,
the one who heard and held the web-frail threads
crept, faltered, crept again and did not dare to stride,
lest in his halting gait the threads should shatter.
His the assignment, to the haunts of men to take the message,
break the code and scatter on word-winds the interpretation:
to hint the Eternal Pulse's beat on stronger wing,
sweet sap rising in the veiled and thin-veined heartstream:
long clenching winter's frostgrip melted, vanished,
the crooked straight, rough places smooth planed,
planished for the New World's Spring.

John Allison

GARDENS

Turn a spit on a February morn
With your favourite spade in hand,
All around nature adorns
The delight of our great land.

From country cottage to stately home
Town terrace to public park,
The delight of gardens to view and roam
Is sure to make its mark.

The snowdrops brighten lawn and home
Whilst spring's not far away,
Soon grass is mown and seeds are sown
Not long 'twill soon be May.

When summer comes and lark's in sky
Whilst veggies and flowers flourish,
It's time for bees and butterflies,
Sights and sounds to cherish.

As daylight hours are on the wane
And swallows leave our land,
The crops are gathered when no rain,
Good food near at hand.

Brian R Russ

Awakening

The dark roof of night is lifting,
Revealing the wondrous upsurge of spring
Which sets the very blood of man a tingling.
The green and brown of beech unfurling,
The very majesty of trees awakening.
Wondrous rhythm of a day, with dark
With light, with in-betweens.
The tender break of dawn,
Slowly showing the blues, the pinks, the whites
Of floral delight, with breathtaking greens
Of every shade,
Surely shows the Creator has not forgotten,
As long winter may seem to indicate.
Oh joy of spring. Oh joy, oh joy, oh joy!

Ted Turl

OMENS OF THE BIRDS

We all appreciate the joy that birds can bring
The cuckoo call proclaims the coming of the spring
Turn your money over . . . You'll have enough to pay
your way . . . until he returns . . . next years new spring day.

I am told that if a quacking duck you should see
(not near water) can denote prosperity
Flying ducks too, promise happier times for you
(makes me wonder if omens really can be true)

If a white dove or pigeon circles the sky
then should it come to rest on your home roof up high
this could indicate for one of your family
very soon a love match or a wedding could be.

Magpies chattering . . . herald unexpected guests
with good news and the promise of happiness
and magpies too can symbolise prosperity
(for this we shall have to wait and see . . . patiently)

If a swallows seen very early in the spring
a happy summer for all . . . this bird will bring
How can we be sad when these birds we hear and see
bring promise of Good Luck and Prosperity.

Valerie Ovais

BLISSFUL SPRING

All is bliss, everything appears beautiful and white -
Gone is winter's blackness, spring has brought such glorious delight!
My dark season's depression has left me,
Spring has cured me and I now see so clearly.

From my eiderdowned bed I see other beautiful, colourful beds
A bed of roses, one of daffodils, bluebells situated closely to my
                                                                  garden shed.
The sun is making a shy entrance and we all encourage it to be bolder
To make a dramatic debut in all its glory, to be much golder.

Spring speaks of better days and nicer things to see and do -
Picnics in the park, visits to the wildlife parks where like Noah's Ark
the animals are in pairs - two,
The occasional rainy days do not bother me as my spirits have already
                                                                    been lifted -
The balance of nature is just right - to happy, hopeful spring it has
                                                                    already shifted.
Spring is a time to hope and dream, working at schemes which we wish
                                                                    shall succeed -
To shed all fears and hold on through thick and thin, but being cautious,
                                                                    taking heed,
A fresh outlook, a zest for life itself, a hold on your reserves
And in time as this season is past your goals will be achieved -
much more, not less than you and I deserve.

Margaret Andrews

Blossoming Brilliance

It's happened! Once again as before
Spring has awoken to rid us of the bore
Of darkened lives and tedious remorse
Caused by winter and its sinister force

Spring has given us breath again
To pump deeply into our lungs, to mend
The depression over the past few months
To vigour our senses toward positive thoughts

Stare outside and admire the life
Of flowers reborn to display their wealth
Of Blossoming Brilliance for all to see
In a crescendo of colour, they announce Spring to me!

Harriet J Kent

SPRINGTIME'S SERENADE

Dawn's spring sky triumphs o'er night,
Scatters winter's gloomy care;
Earth renewed, daisies' delight,
Raptured bird-song fills the air.
Sportive lambs frisk, jump at play,
With gladness in lusty May.

Bluebells, orchids, columbine,
Herald the wonder of spring.
Babbling brook and celandine,
Grateful thanks and blessings bring.
South-west winds from providence,
Faith's stronghold our sure defence.

March sowing, breeding season,
Jack raced to clinic in car.
'Baby's due that's the reason,
I've timed how long to bring Ma'
Nurse snapped 'Bring her instantly,
Drive your fast Bentley gently.'

Sally came with suddenness,
Newborn length twenty inches,
Seven pounds of joyousness,
Mum's arms around her clinches.
Between feeds the baby sleeps,
In sunny fresh air she peeps.

Springtime's sparkling scallop shells,
Periwinkles from seaweed;
Pink cowries are seashore belles,
With cockles, dog whelks, rockweed.
Scallop shell is pilgrim's gage,
Truth's immortal heritage.

James Leonard Clough

HOPE AFRESH

Time for the lamb to leap the sunbeam
Birds sing when getting up and before feathered dream
And fish return to river and meadow stream
The green carpet is spread and blossoms sunlit gleam
Snowdrops nod approval and daffodils trumpet their call
To mark resurrection through to the fall
And all that's new gives hope afresh
To all mortals in the flesh
Following dreams and seeking spirits
Woven in life's mysterious mesh.

Clive Cornwall

NATURE'S GIFTS

The transformation from winter to spring,
A glorious awakening as new life begins.
An explosion of miracles has occurred overnight
Confronting our eyes, a magical sight.

Interspersed in meadows are welcome spring flowers,
Hastened to blossom by sunshine and showers,
Trees stark, bare branches now swathed in green
For nesting birds, a protective screen.

Swallows arrive to nurture their young
From thousands of miles, the breeding's begun
The lazy cuckoo, an egg she does lay
In another birds nest, it's nature's way.

Dragonflies with brilliant wings,
Bright colours to the pond they bring.
Whilst frogs croak to attract a mate
Anxious to spawn before it's too late.

As twilight descends, the fox leaves his earth
She needs to catch rabbits as she's just given birth
Families of hedgehogs scamper around
Owls flying overhead with never a sound.

Springtime is special, a time of rebirth
We must not take for granted this wonderful earth,
To protect nature's gifts is a vital role,
If we all work together we'll achieve our goal.

D E Kowalska

SPRING RITES

Fertility, fertility
It's time to show virility
The sap is rising
Spring has sprung
The trees have got new dresses on

Maternity, maternity
The field's a sheep infirmary
The lambs are popping
Out to see
The birds build homes in every tree

Polygamy, polygamy
It's hard to stick to two or three
When nature screams
'Let's multiply
It's time to reproduce'

Domesticity it's plain to see
Is not winter's activity
The sun is shining
Let's make hay
We'll spring clean another day

Carolyn McDonald

APPLE BLOSSOM

High up our cottage gardens grew the trees,
No formal orchard this, in age or line,
But freely planted, open to the breeze,
My neighbours' houses hidden, theirs and mine.
Three hundred years and more since those were new,
From local quarries hewn, to shelter folk
There born, wed, working, yes and dying too,
Neighbourly sharing tidings as they broke.
And pink and white grew apple blossom sweet,
Bridal against the spring's translucent sky,
And daisied grass was soft beneath my feet,
And all was rich with bee and butterfly.
Hard-trampled over all the many years
By dry-stone wall our footpath climbs the hill.
Between the trees an unknown friend appears
While 'Ginger' roams the orchard as he will.
He comes with loving croon to greet me there,
And as I stoop to stroke his silken head -
Sudden I wake, and know not anywhere
Was apple blossom in my garden spread.
Long years ago we left, Ginger and I,
And Katie with us; happy in our home
We lived together - why then should I cry
For those lost gardens where they used to roam?
And yet so sweet a dream, so strangely clear!
Does memory (despite my Midland race)
Of apple blossom last three hundred year
And, time-linked, still perfume its dwelling place?

Kathleen M Hatton

THE NEW BEGINNING

Shades of green beginning to show,
tiny leaf buds on every tree,
freshly woken after the snow,
spring flowers fighting to be free.

Each morning bringing fresh delight
as frost begins to fade away,
dispelling shadows of the night,
the eyes behold this brand new day.

Birds now bursting into song,
soon they'll have no time to rest,
nature warns it will not be long
before they need a larger nest.

The sheep and cattle roaming round
waiting, restless to give new birth,
the air now filled with constant sound,
the musty smell of burrowed earth.

To cross the field and climb the stile,
pass by the bluebell wood,
the urge to ramble many a mile,
enjoying spring while I could.

Joiann

Roddy

Roddy a man of thought,
A mind full of will and staggering thought,
A life always fighting to live for any reason,
Biding time, waiting for the chance
To steal the wind from the blowing breeze,
To take that moment that will change all,
For he waits to seal his fate,
To be the bloom upon the breeze.

K M Clemo

LAKELAND WILD FLOWERS

Lakeland blossom so radiant this day
gladdens the eyes as a wedding bouquet.
Exalted foxglove attired in pristine white,
curtsies to scarlet rose with visible delight.

Buttercups, daisies and cornflower blue,
unite with sunny primrose to form a blissful queue.

Purple carpet clover stretches nigh a mile,
and nudge the blood red poppies
with a gentle loving smile.

Alex Branthwaite

NATURE'S TREASURES

Ancient woodland,
Where rare flowers bloom
Oaks stand proud and tall.
Drystone walls stand test of time!
Skylarks singing with joy.
Gentle breeze scatters acorn seeds,
Snowdrops hanging like church bells,
Fragrant cherry blossom fills the air.
Speckled tinted wild orchid brings joy to a smiling face.

A Hattersley

SINGING WORLDS
(To Blackie)

(And through it all the little birdie sang)

It mattered not
Sun's smile had slipped
Now chaos reigned
For here in life
This was a balanced
Sweet refrain
Though nature's vision - taught of singing worlds set free
Dynamic was the force
Adhered to pure simplicity.

Irene Gunnion

TWENTY SECOND SCENE

I stared at evening's pencil trees
Severely sketched in putty sky
When shafts of red transformed the sight
As skinny birds in sweeping flight
Shone silver through the blue.

Sculptured in a shifting rose,
Swirling gold autumnal light,
Ginger trees so lofty, proud
Softly kissing crumbling clouds
Changing form and hue.

Instantly the scene was spoiled
Grey on grey. Soiling light.
Plunging air degrees below,
For shrouded birds in eerie glow
- A memory in flight.

Patricia Holland

DAWNING BEAUTY

As we talk, I look into your eyes
forbidding my heart and mind to agree
unsure of the result.
The care, the concern in your eyes
making me feel beautiful
causes me to weep.

I dare not speak my thoughts aloud
or voice the desires of my heart
unsure of what I want.
The feeling caused by simple words,
a look that says so much
brings me joy.

A hopefulness springs in my soul,
a dawning of reality and truth
sure of who I am and can be.
Your look and your words show
despite everything and everyone
I can be beautiful.

Sarah Bradley

SO NEAR MY HEART

My dearly beloved, mine own heart's desire,
Tell me you love me, set me afire.
Afire with the touch of your kisses so sweet.
Abeat with embraces to make my heart beat.
Abeat with the thought you are ever near.
Astir with the thought you are always here.
Yet how to finish this to you I don't know quite,
'For dearest,' I do think of you, by day and by night,
So 'Dear one,' think of me while we are apart,
For you are the one ,
'So near to my heart.'

D G Hill

SUBMISSIONS INVITED
SOMETHING FOR EVERYONE

POETRY NOW '99 - Any subject, any style, any time.

WOMENSWORDS '99 - Strictly women, have your say the female way!

STRONGWORDS '99 - Warning! Age restriction, must be between 16-24, opinionated and have strong views. (Not for the faint-hearted)

All poems no longer than 30 lines.
Always welcome! No fee!
Cash Prizes to be won!

Mark your envelope (eg *Poetry Now*) **'99**
Send to:
Forward Press Ltd
Remus House, Coltsfoot Drive,
Woodston,
Peterborough, PE2 9JX

OVER £10,000 POETRY PRIZES TO BE WON!

Judging will take place in October 1999